Compassion Series

FOREWORD BY THE HONOURABLE

IT'S HARD NOT TO STARE

HELPING CHILDREN UNDERSTAND DISABILITIES

WRITTEN & ILLUSTRATED BY TIM HUFF

PARENT & TEACHER DISCUSSION GUIDE BY JAN FUKUMOTO

CASTLE QUAY BOOKS
WWW.CASTLEQUAYBOOKS.COM

It's Hard Not To Stare: Helping Children Understand Disabilities
Copyright ©2013 Tim J Huff
All rights reserved
Printed in Canada
International Standard Book Number 978-1-927355-28-2
ISBN 978-1-927355-29-9 EPUB

Published by:
Castle Quay Books
Pickering, Ontario, L1W 1A5
Tel: (416) 573-3249
E-mail: info@castlequaybooks.com   www.castlequaybooks.com

Cover art by Tim J Huff
Discussion guide by Jan Fukumoto
Cover and interior design by Diane Roblin Lee, ByDesign Media   www.bydesignmedia.ca
Printed at Essence Publishing, Belleville, Ontario

This book or parts thereof may not be reproduced in any form without prior written permission of the publishers.

Library and Archives Canada Cataloguing in Publication

Huff, Tim, 1964-, author, illustrator
        It's hard not to stare : helping children understand disabilities
/ written & illustrated by Tim Huff ; foreword by the Honourable
David C. Onley ; parent & teacher discussion guide by Jan Fukumoto.

(Compassion series ; 2)
Issued in print and electronic formats.
ISBN 978-1-927355-28-2 (pbk)--ISBN 978-1-927355-29-9 (epub)

        1. People with disabilities--Juvenile literature. 2. Compassion--
Juvenile literature. I. Fukumoto, Jan, 1958-, author of discussion
guide II. Title.

HV1568.H83 2013   j362.4   C2013-905365-4
                                          C2013-906113-4

FOREWORD

As Ontario's first Lieutenant Governor with a physical disability, I adopted accessibility as the overarching theme of my term of office. I defined accessibility as that which enables people to achieve their full potential.

I chose this definition because I wanted people to understand that while the ubiquitous blue and white wheelchair symbol shows the location of physically accessible facilities, it doesn't mean that all barriers to accessibility have been removed. While such things as ramps, automatic doors and wheelchair parking spots have helped people with disabilities greatly, another kind of barrier still stubbornly remains.

In fact, the barrier that most often affects people with disabilities is not physical or part of their own condition. It is instead attitudinal, other people's attitudes.

Over the years in various speeches, I have asked this question: "When you meet someone with a disability for the first time, what do you see; their disability or their ability within?"

We'd all like to say we see the ability because it's an answer that makes us feel good. But we all know that is not true: we all see the disability. And there's nothing wrong with that as long as we don't let the first glance become a longer look that then becomes a stare, a negative opinion or value judgment on the person.

Tim Huff's *It's Hard Not to Stare: Helping Children Understand Disabilities* is a remarkable contribution to the dialogue that is taking us closer and closer to being a fully accessible society. He does this through words and images that gently, respectfully but bluntly pose questions and observations about people with disabilities. Words like: "It's hard not to stare at some people, sometimes. Are they okay? Will they be fine?"

In the end, important lessons are conveyed for children and as important, for all of us too.

People with a whole range of disabilities are portrayed as fully functioning members of society who are only really handicapped if other people judge them negatively.

Tim Huff's words and illustrations touch our hearts and minds, guiding children forward from staring to caring. In this he appeals to our better selves and in so doing helps make us all a better, more compassionate and loving people.

David C. Onley, O.Ont.
Lieutenant Governor of Ontario

A MESSAGE FROM THE AUTHOR...

to parents, teachers and caregivers

When I was 16 years old, I naively volunteered to serve at a unique camp for deaf and disabled children—The Bob Rumball Camp of the Deaf. The impact of this decision was extraordinary and set me on an unpredictable life journey filled with profound meaning, adventure and mystery. And while I have striven to serve well throughout my life and full-time career among people who have so often felt categorized, stigmatized and marginalized, I am overwhelmingly humbled by how I have been continuously blessed in their midst. Even as this book is released, I am extremely sensitive to the fact that words and definitions—socially, culturally and professionally—change so rapidly. A great many of the words and definitions at the centre of my own formal developmental service worker education long ago and within the various agencies that I've been associated with over the years are now considered nothing shy of "wrong." Even as this book is released using the word "disabilities," I wonder how long that moniker will be considered socially or politically correct. Yet my prayer is that the heartbeat and tenor of this book will sustain its value in the years to come, regardless of the ever-changing language.

Ultimately, I believe that when we nurture compassion in a child for one area of life, the potential is great that this goodness will spill over into all other areas. Teaching, modelling and discussing the principles and values of understanding, compassion and service, can and will, impact the social framework of generations to come. And what our children reveal in the process, teaching us in return, is most often extraordinary.

Much has occurred since Castle Quay Books published my first children's book, *The Cardboard Shack Beneath the Bridge: Helping Children Understand Homelessness*, in 2006. That book went on to become an award-winning bestseller and the impetus for the development of a children's "Compassion Series" program within the registered charity I co-founded in 2012 called StreetLevel (http://www.streetlevel.ca).

Between the release of my first children's book and this one, Castle Quay Books has also published two adult books I've written, *Bent Hope* and *Dancing with Dynamite*, that have likewise been more successful than I could have imagined—with more writing projects in the works for children and adults. All of these books, including this one, ultimately have the same purpose in my heart and mind: that all who read them would know that we are all cherished by a loving God and meant to cherish one another. It is with great respect for those of differing theologies and philosophies and for those gathered in the settings where this book might arrive (schools, agencies, homes) that I am careful to never force these tender beliefs on anyone. At the same time, I wouldn't want anyone to be left wondering about the heartbeat that enlivens the books.

All the best,

AUTHORS' ACKNOWLEDGEMENTS

With several books published at this point, all with detailed author's acknowledgements, and with limited space available here, to my dear and supportive friends—know that your names are as alive now in my heart and mind as ever, as I give thanksgiving. However, I do need to acknowledge the dear friends who contributed feedback and insight specific to this project throughout the process: Nanci and Steve Bell, Annie Brandner, Laura Jane Brew, Cathy Dienesch, Jocelyn Durston, Susie and Tim Griffin, Jodi and Mike Janzen, Sarah Lester, Jennine Loewen, Lori and John McAuley, Debbie and Don Morrison, Sister Sue Mosteller, Greg Paul, Angela Porter, Annie Robins, Derek Rumball, Ruth Smith, Brenda Tennant, Lori Ward, Trish and John Wilkinson.

What an honour to have experienced the ongoing kindness and encouragement of the Honourable David. C. Onley while crafting this special book.

It has been, and is, such a gift to work alongside my friend Jan Fukumoto. Integrity and wisdom of this calibre are so rare.

I continue to be endlessly blessed by Larry and Marina Willard and Castle Quay Books. I thank God everyday!

Once again, I am so humbled by the goodness of Miller and Terri Alloway and the Maranatha Foundation. Likewise by Brad and Kelly Pedersen and the Tech4Kids team.

Special thanks, as always, to my dear friend Julia Beazley for the countless ways she assists in bringing my writing projects to life. Likewise, I am so appreciative of the kinship and support from the rest of the StreetLevel family: Alison Hardman, Pat Nixon, our excellent board of directors and the renowned members of the National StreetLevel Advisory.

I would be remiss if I did not mention my great and personal affection for L'Arche Daybreak and the Bob Rumball Camp (and Associations) for the Deaf, in gratitude of the spirit, learning and opportunities they have afforded me.

To my parents, my brothers and their families, and the extended Johnson family—thank you for your continuous love and support. No words do justice to my own beloved and loving family who fill me up everyday: Diane, Sarah Jane, Jake.

Tim Huff

Thank you to my colleagues at the Toronto District School Board, particularly those in the Special Education Department and on the Autism Services Team. Not only do I appreciate your input on this book but I also value your partnership in accessing the best for all students and families that we work with. I cannot imagine doing my job without you.

My biggest teachers have been my students and their families as well as my friends with an Autism Spectrum Disorder. You have challenged me to see beyond your differences and respect you for the amazing individuals who you are. Jason and Kaitrin, you continue to be an inspiration to me in all that I do.

The biggest thank you goes to my own children, Johnny and Jen, Sarah and Erin who continue to challenge me to be the best I can be and to my husband who loves and accepts me everyday. Love you more.

Jan Fukumoto

IT'S HARD NOT TO
STARE

BREATHE
BRAVR
RESPECT
FAMILIAR
INCLUDE
CEREBRAL
SUPPORT
LOOK
PROSTHESIS
MOBILITY
ABILITY

It's hard not to stare
at some people, sometimes.

Are they okay?
Will they be fine?

It's hard not to wonder what life might be like to not skip a rope or not ride a bike.

It's hard not to watch people talk with their hands, making words in a way you don't understand.

It's hard to imagine how dark it might be or how it would feel if you couldn't see.

There is a word
that often is used
It means many things
but don't be confused.

The word is "disabled,"
but as you will see
it's just about people
like you and like me.

Perhaps there is something that's simple for you, that wouldn't be easy for others to do.

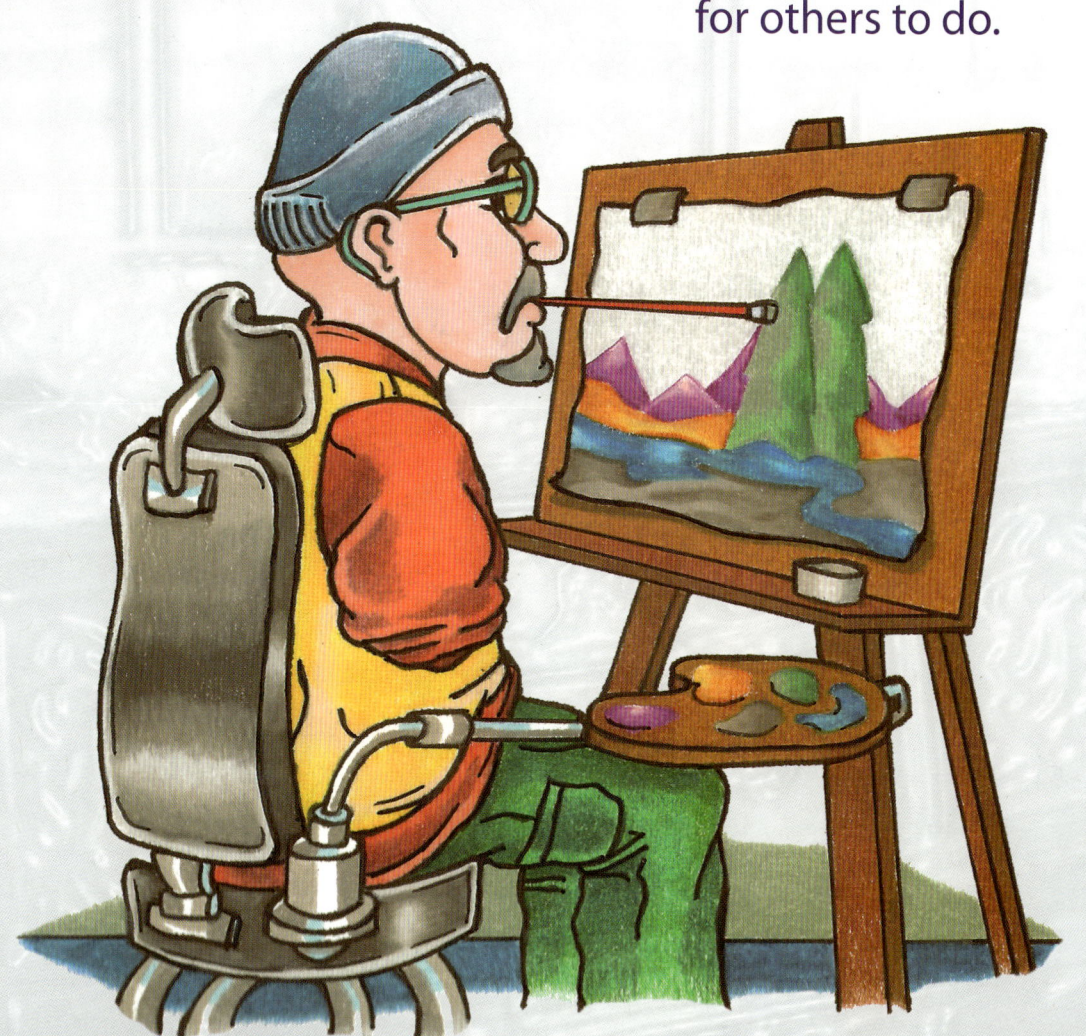

Some people bravely must find other ways to learn, get around, to speak or to play.

Some people live with bodies and minds that may need some help or take extra time.

Some people shake
or their bodies don't move in ways they might hope—
simple and smooth.

Challenge may come at birth or old age, or injury and illness at some other stage.

There's one other word
you also should know;
A word that will help
as you learn and you grow.

The word is "familiar." Quite simply it means something you're used to or have already seen.

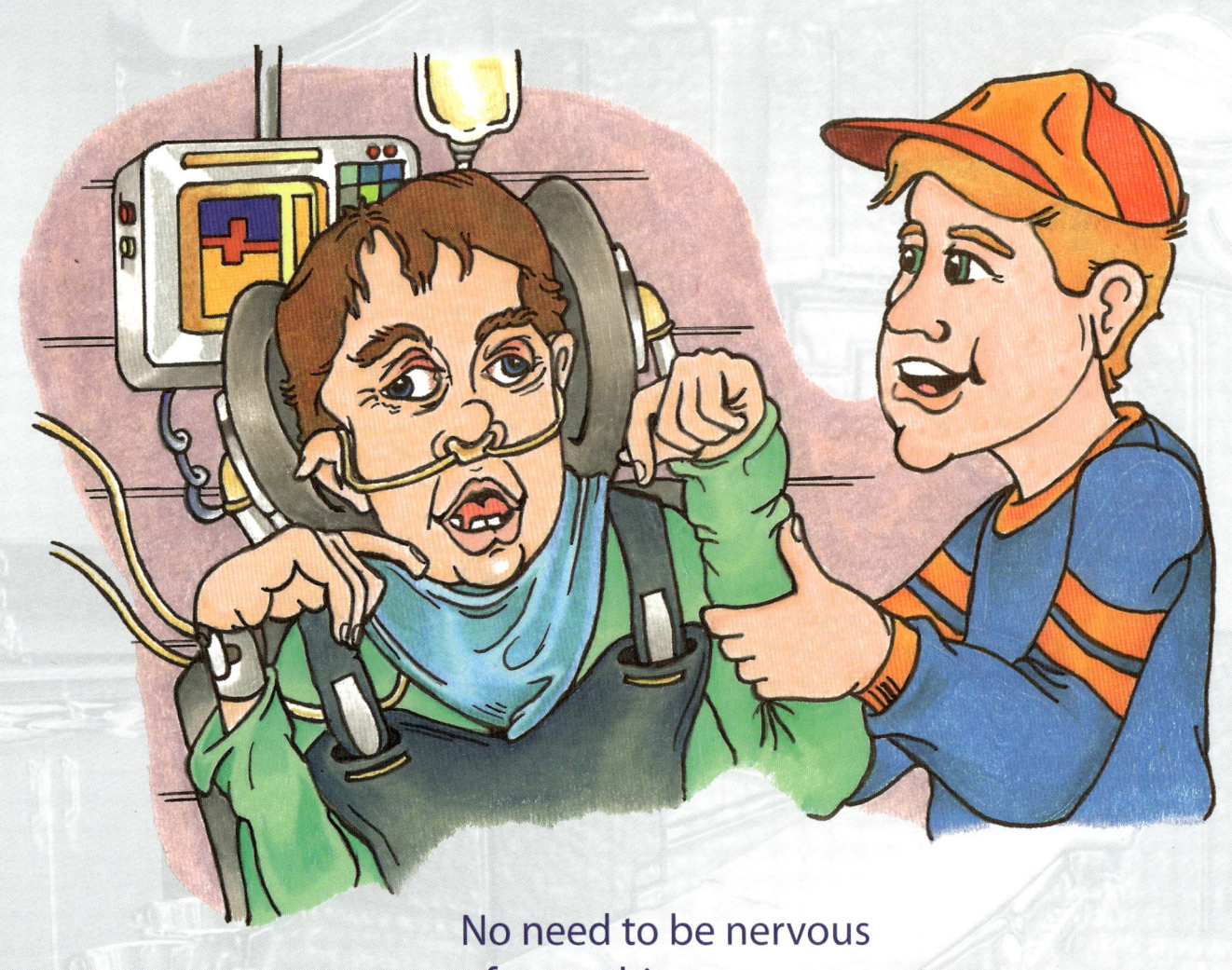

No need to be nervous
of something you see
when you can say,
"It's familiar to me."

24

So look with your eyes
but then do your part;
Be kind with your questions;
Look with your heart.

And don't be afraid to wonder or ask
if you can help with some simple task.

Soon you will find
it's **not** hard not to stare.
But mostly you'll find
it's hard not to care.

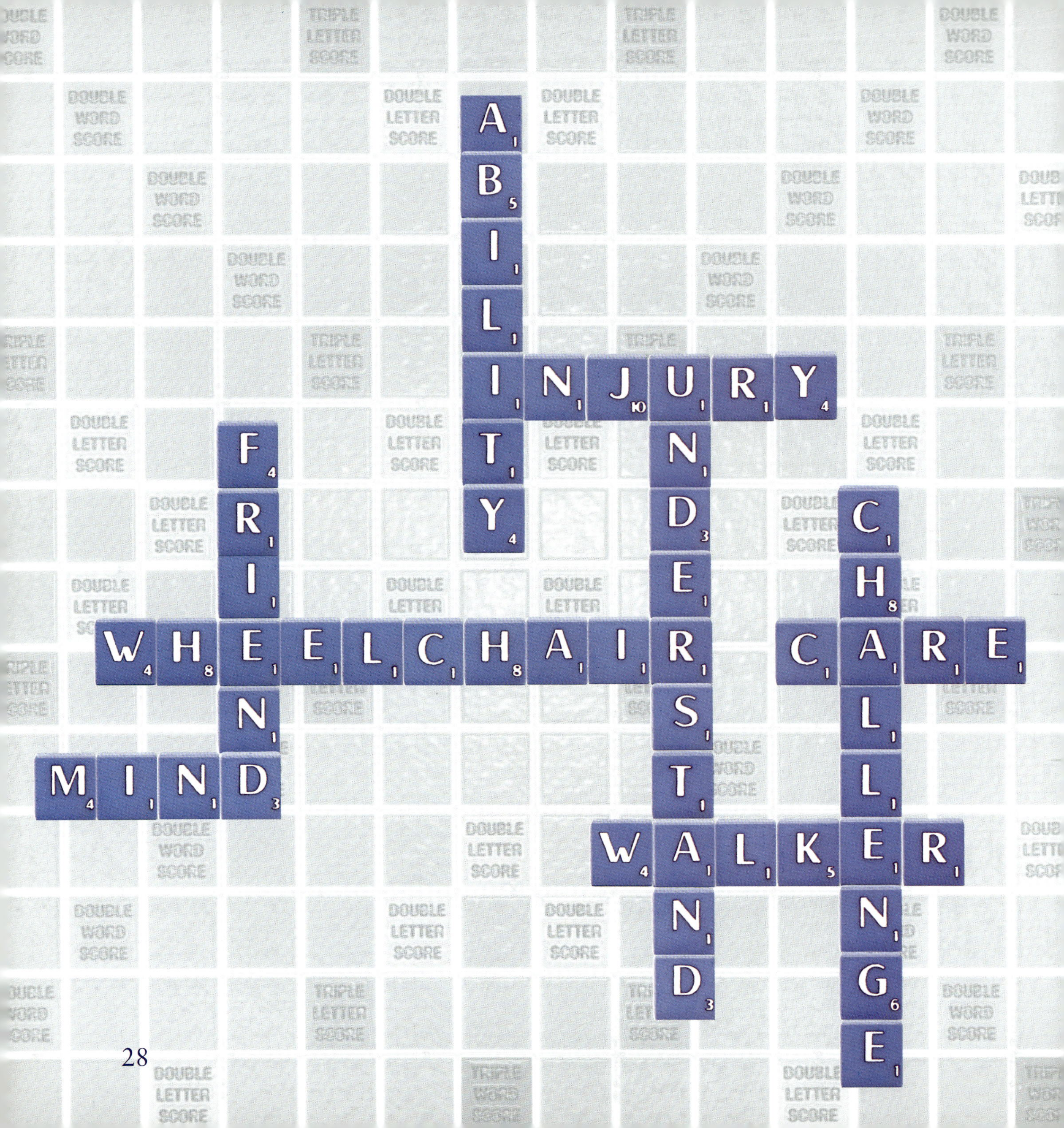
ABILITY
INJURY
UNDERSTAND
FRIEND
WHEELCHAIR
CARE
CHALLENGE
MIND
WALKER

SHARING PAGES

A Discussion Guide for Parents, Teachers and Caregivers

Page-By-Page Discussion and Helps

Have you ever stared at an individual and then quickly looked away when the person caught your eye? Or do you remember an adult whispering to you as a child, "Don't stare. That's rude?" Most of us remember the awkwardness or even the guilt of these experiences. The purpose of the guide is to support you in encouraging children to ask questions and to replace the awkwardness with understanding and caring.

Notes for educators, parents and grandparents:

1. You don't need to know all the answers.
Acknowledge when you need to get more information.
"That's a great question. I will find out the right answer for you."

2. Know the personal experiences of your audience.
Involve children who have firsthand experience with disabilities. Read the book with them ahead of time and ask for their input before reading the book with the larger group.

3. Use "person-first" language.

4. Talk about the girl who is visually impaired or the boy with autism, as opposed to the blind girl or the autistic boy. This puts value on the person rather than emphasis on the disability.

5. Read the story from beginning to end and then use the children's questions to guide your discussion. Children will ask what they need to know or are ready to hear.

6. The questions are phrased specifically for children. Some of the additional comments and information are framed to be educational for adults and children, providing knowledge that adults can adapt appropriately for various ages.

Discussion Guide prepared and written by Jan Fukumoto.

Jan Fukumoto is highly respected and uniquely experienced in the field of education, having worked or volunteered for more than three decades almost exclusively with students with exceptionalities. Currently she works for the Toronto District School Board in the role of Central Coordinator of Autism Services. She is also a member of the founding board of directors for The Hope Exchange StreetLevel Network; known primarily as "StreetLevel." Jan is married to Bob and they are the parents of three adult children.

DISCUSSION STARTERS

Page 11 - What is one thing you notice in the picture?
    (Be prepared that it may not be the man's leg.)
    What do you think happened to the man's leg?
    What are the boys thinking?

Crutches are used to help people walk when their legs don't work like they need them to. It looks like this man does not have all of one leg. Maybe he was born like this, maybe he was in an accident or maybe he has a disease that hurt his leg. An amputee is someone who has an arm or leg removed to stop the pain or disease from spreading. He still likes to go outside and walk so he uses his crutches.

Page 12 - There is a girl standing.
    What is she planning on doing?
    How can the girl in the wheelchair join her?
    What else could they play together?

The wheelchair only stops the girl from playing with the other girl if they aren't open to changing the game. If we accommodate or change things, everyone can play.

Page 13 - Why are these men talking with their hands?
    What would you miss the most if you could not hear?
    How could you talk to a friend who is deaf?

People who have difficulty hearing may be hard of hearing or deaf. Sometimes people use hearing aids to help them hear; they may also read lips or use Sign Language. (This would be an excellent time to teach a few simple signs to your children. Begin with "friend," "help," "please" and "thank you." There are great videos and pictures on the Internet that you can use.)

Page 14 - Why is this man walking with a dog?
How does the dog know what to do?
Have you ever seen someone with an assistance dog?

People who have difficulty seeing may have a visual impairment. They may be blind or have low vision.

Assistance Dogs are trained to help many people, including those who are deaf, have an Autism Spectrum Disorder or are visually impaired. When the dog is wearing a harness or a vest, it is working and needs to concentrate on its work. Just like with any dog, you should not play with or pet the dog unless you first ask the owner.

Page 15 - What do you notice about the blocks? (Perhaps that they are being stacked up identically.)

Autism Spectrum Disorder (ASD) is a neurological disorder, meaning that the brain of a person with an ASD is wired differently. The person's brain often doesn't give them the right signals about what is going on around them. It may be difficult for them to talk or it may be hard for them to stop talking about their favourite topic. They may be very sensitive to loud noises, bright lights or funny smells. They may insist on doing the same thing over and over again and find it very hard when things around them change. It may also mean that they have extra smarts in a special area like math, music or art. Autism Spectrum Disorder looks very different in every individual, but all of these differences can make it hard for someone with an ASD to make friends. If you have classmates or neighbours with an ASD, remember that just like you, they want to make friends and be respected for who they are.

Page 16 - How many of you have been camping?
Who knows how to play an instrument?
Who likes roasted marshmallows?

We are all more alike than we are different. It looks like everyone is having a great time at the campfire.

Page 17 - What is the man painting?
   Why is he painting with the brush in his mouth?
   Are you surprised the man still wants to paint when it is such hard work?

When people are paralyzed from illness or an accident, they cannot move their arms or their legs or sometimes both. There are many famous mouth artists who paint with brushes in their mouths. They love to paint so they discover a different way to paint in order to continue to do what they want to do. Even though his body does not move well, the man still sees the art in his mind that he wants to create.

Page 18 - What sport is this?
   Why are they not skating using their feet?
   What is a physical disability?

Sledge or sled hockey is a sport that allows individuals with a physical disability to play hockey. It is a sport in the Paralympics.

The Paralympic Games is a large sporting event like the Olympics that involves athletes with a wide range of physical and intellectual disabilities. They compete for medals against athletes from other countries all around the world.

Physical disability is a term used to describe someone that has difficultly moving their body in the same way that you and I move our bodies.

Intellectual disability is a term used to describe someone that learns differently and may need more time to learn new things.

Page 19 - How is the sister helping her brother?
   Why can't the brother do it himself? Isn't he too old to need help?
   This wheelchair has a tray on it—why is that?

Sometimes people need help with things that are easy for us. It must be very hard to need someone to feed you when you are older. You could feel like you are being treated like a baby. His sister is helping in a way that is kind. A word that describes this is dignity or respect. The sister believes that her brother is just as important as she is, even though he cannot eat on his own, so she treats him kindly, with dignity and respect.

Page 20 - This young man may appear that he is not sitting in his wheelchair properly. Sometimes his body does not do what he wants it to do. His arms and legs go stiff or straight. How would that feel?

The boy in the wheelchair may have Cerebral Palsy. The word cerebral means having to do with the brain. The word palsy means a weakness in the way a person moves or positions his or her body. If the brain is not able to tell the body exactly what to do, someone with Cerebral Palsy may not be able to talk, walk or move the way you do. Just like you and I, all people with Cerebral Palsy are different but they want to do many of the same activities. You can help by understanding that it may take a friend with Cerebral Palsy longer to do some of the things you do with them.

Page 21 - What does the older woman have in front of her?
Why does she need it?
Has she always needed it?

People have physical challenges for different reasons, like growing older, injury or illness.

A walker is a piece of equipment that gives you support when you are walking when your body does not work like you want it to.

Page 22 - What does this picture tell you?

You may recognize some people as having Down syndrome. You can usually tell because they have different facial features. A person with Down syndrome is born with an extra chromosome inside the cells of their body. This extra chromosome can make it more challenging for them to talk, walk or think as quickly as you do. They will always have Down syndrome, but will learn to do things faster and better as they grow older.

Page 23 - Can you tell what is happening in this picture?
   Who is helping the man?
   Why does he need help?

A prosthesis is an artificial device that replaces a body part and helps it work like the original part. Medical professionals help to make sure it fits properly and works well.

Page 24 - These two boys are brothers. What do you think they are talking about?
   What can you tell by the face of the brother who is standing up?

Sometimes children and adults need special equipment to help them do things like breathe or eat. It can be scary when we don't know what the equipment is for. The brother who is standing is not afraid. He is happy to be with his brother. He understands that the oxygen tube and other equipment are helping his brother. He is really happy to be able to visit and talk with him.

Page 25 - What do you see in this picture?
   How does this picture make you feel?

Being without a home is very difficult. It is even more challenging for people who also have disabilities. It is possible that the man in this picture lost his legs because of a disease or an injury after he became homeless. There are many dedicated individuals and agencies who support and care for people who are homeless. They do their best to provide special care for those with disabilities.

For more information about groups working with individuals who are homeless, go to http://www.streetlevel.ca

To teach children more about homelessness, check out Tim Huff's first children's book, *The Cardboard Shack Beneath The Bridge: Helping Children Understand Homelessness* (published by Castle Quay Books).

Page 26 - What is this girl doing?
　　　　　Does the man need help?

A mobility scooter is a vehicle like a wheelchair that is power operated and helps people go places when their legs don't work like they need them to.

Page 27 - How are the children the same?
　　　　　How are they different?

The illustration is created in a way that puts the child with the biggest difference at the centre, surrounded by those with other differences. When we stop staring, we look for ways to care.

FROM STARING TO CARING

If we are unfamiliar with other people's differences, we may stare at them, be afraid or even avoid them.

If we are familiar and feel like we can ask questions, we may accept, involve and care for others, regardless of their differences.

For more information about StreetLevel and the Compassion Series visit www.streetlevel.ca